CIVIC PARTICIPATION
Working for Civil Rights

AMERICAN INDIAN RIGHTS
MOVEMENT

Sarah Machajewski

PowerKiDS press.

New York

Published in 2017 by The Rosen Publishing Group, Inc.
29 East 21st Street, New York, NY 10010

First Edition

Editor: Caitie McAneney
Book Design: Mickey Harmon

Photo Credits: Cover (image) Pictorial Parade/Archive Photos/Getty Images; cover, pp. 1, 3–32 (background) Milena_Bo/Shutterstock.com; pp. 5, 9 Image courtesy of the Library of Congress; p. 7 Encyclopaedia Britannica/UIG/Getty Images; p. 10 https://en.wikipedia.org/wiki/American_Indian_boarding_schools#/media/File:Chiricahua_Apaches_Four_Months_After_Arriving_at_Carlisle.jpg; p. 11 https://en.wikipedia.org/wiki/Treaty_of_Fort_Laramie_(1868)#/media/File:Photograph_of_General_William_T._Sherman_and_Commissioners_in_Council_with_Indian_Chiefs_at_Fort_Laramie,_Wyoming,_ca._1_-_NARA_-_531079.jpg; p. 13 https://en.wikipedia.org/wiki/National_Congress_of_American_Indians#/media/File:Representatives_of_various_tribes_attending_organizational_meeting_of_the_National_Congress_of_American_Indians..._-_NARA_-_298658.jpg; pp. 15, 17, 19, 21, 23, 25 Bettmann/Contributor/Bettmann/Getty Images; p. 22 Ralph Crane/Contributor/The LIFE Picture Collection/Getty Images; p. 27 Education Images/Contributor/Universal Images Group/Getty Images; p. 29 NICHOLAS KAMM/Staff/AFP/Getty Images.

Library of Congress Cataloging-in-Publication Data

Names: Machajewski, Sarah, author.
Title: American Indian rights movement / Sarah Machajewski.
Description: New York : PowerKids Press, 2017. | Series: Civic participation: Working for civil rights | Includes index.
Identifiers: LCCN 2016037062| ISBN 9781499426755 (pbk. book) | ISBN 9781499426786 (6 pack) | ISBN 9781499428490 (library bound book)
Subjects: LCSH: Indians of North America-Politics and government-Juvenile literature. | Indians of North America-Government relations-Juvenile literature. | Indians of North America-Civil rights-Juvenile literature. | Red Power movement-United States-Juvenile literature. | American Indian Movement-Juvenile literature. | Indians, Treatment of-United States-Juvenile literature.
Classification: LCC E93 .M113 2017 | DDC 323.1197-dc23
LC record available at https://lccn.loc.gov/2016037062

Manufactured in the United States of America

CPSIA Compliance Information: Batch #BW17PK: For Further Information contact Rosen Publishing, New York, New York at 1-800-237-9932

CONTENTS

FIGHTING FOR WHAT'S LOST

In 1776, leaders of the American colonies signed the Declaration of Independence, which announced to the world that "all men are created equal." History has shown that it's far more **complicated** than that. In the United States, many groups of people have faced discrimination, or have been treated unfairly.

American Indian peoples have been discriminated against by Europeans since Europeans arrived in the Americas. For centuries, they watched their people die at the hands of white men and they suffered as their lands and rights were taken away. Gradually, a movement was organized to try to take back what had been lost. This movement drew national attention to the injustices American Indians experience. Today, people are still fighting to right the wrongs American Indians have suffered.

In this 1978 photo, a tepee sits in the shadow of the Washington Monument as part of a protest.

What Is Discrimination?

Discrimination is unfair treatment based on somebody's race, age, gender, disability, or other factors. People are discriminated against when they're seen as "different." They may be seen this way because of their skin color, the religion they practice, or whom they love. Discrimination happens in everyday life and, sadly, in the courtroom. In the United States, many laws were passed that made discrimination legal. **Activist** groups have worked very hard to reverse these laws so all people will be treated equally.

THE FIRST PEOPLE OF THE AMERICAS

The history of American Indians can be traced back thousands of years. Their **ancestors** have lived in North America for close to 15,000 years. Many **anthropologists** believe those ancestors crossed a land bridge from Asia and settled across the continent. This group of people lost contact with each other over time and hundreds of separate **cultures** developed independently. These people were the first to occupy the Americas.

While American Indians may share common ancestors, each culture has its own set of traditions, beliefs, and ways of life. For thousands of years, tribal nations had their own systems of government and social order. Life existed this way for most cultures until the 15th century, when Europeans crossed an ocean to claim the land as their own.

Today, the land bridge used by ancestors of American Indians is covered by water. Sea levels rose and covered the land thousands of years ago, after the last ice age.

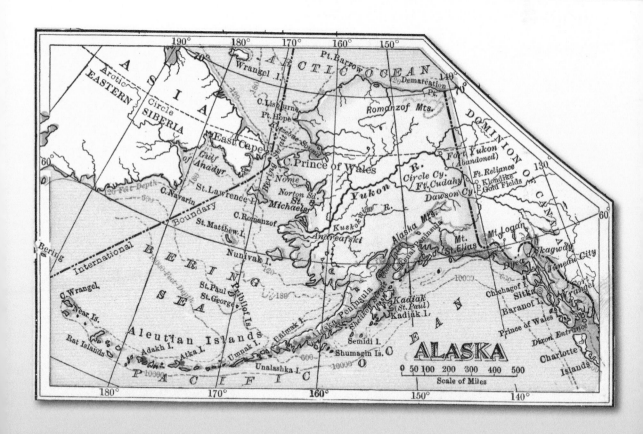

EUROPEANS ARRIVE

When Europeans arrived in the Americas, they thought they had discovered an unknown and unoccupied land. Instead, they found people with highly developed cultures. They called these people "Indians." Europeans called the land the "New World," although it was new only to them.

Life for American Indians changed forever after Europeans arrived. The Europeans brought horses, guns, and sicknesses such as smallpox. Thousands of American Indians died from these unfamiliar threats. As the Europeans established colonies, Indian nations were defeated and the people were forced to give up their lands. Their power and freedoms were slowly stripped away by wars and **treaties**. In time, the white population outnumbered the American Indian population. American Indians became a **minority** group in the land that first belonged to them.

THE JUDGE.

UNCLE SAM'S
PET
HANDS OFF

This political cartoon from 1885 shows an American Indian man as a snake that's squeezing a white family to death while being fed by Uncle Sam, a symbol of the U.S. government. In the background, American Indians attack a white settlement. This cartoon is racist and discriminatory, as it portrays American Indians in a cartoonish and negative light.

Using the Right Language

According to the U.S. Bureau of Indian Affairs, "American Indian" and "Alaska Native" are both preferred terms for people who belong to a federally recognized tribe in the United States. "Native American" became popular in the 1970s. According to the U.S. Bureau of Indian Affairs, that term describes "all Native peoples of the United States and its territories, including American Indians, Alaska Natives, Native Hawaiians, Chamorros, and American Samoans, as well as persons from Canada First Nations and . . . communities in Mexico and Central and South America who are U.S. residents."

BROKEN PROMISES

As the United States expanded west, white settlers pushed American Indians off their lands. The U.S. government accomplished this, in part, through treaties that American Indians were forced to sign. Many treaties stated that American Indian groups would give up their land in exchange for smaller areas of land west of the Mississippi River. These pieces of land were called reservations.

Forced to Fit In

Historically, American Indians have been forced to assimilate to, or fit in with, white society. Between 1880 and 1902, as many as 30,000 American Indian children were removed from their homes and forced to attend boarding schools that were often thousands of miles away. They weren't allowed to speak their native language, practice their traditional beliefs, or wear traditional clothing. They were given new names and forced to learn how to fit in with white society. This terrible form of discrimination separated American Indian children from their families and homes in an attempt to erase their true cultural identity.

From 1778 to 1871, the relationship between the U.S. government and tribal nations existed mainly through treaties. Many treaties are still in effect today. Pictured here is General William T. Sherman and his commissioners signing a peace treaty with Sioux chiefs in Laramie, Wyoming, in 1868.

The U.S. government began establishing reservations after 1778. Throughout the 1800s, millions of Indians were forcibly removed from their lands and relocated to lands in what are now Oklahoma, South Dakota, and Arizona, as well as other territories in the West. Conditions on reservations were terrible. People suffered from lack of food, proper clothing, and housing. They didn't receive the resources and support they were promised. The U.S. government had broken many of its treaties.

THE BEGINNING OF A MOVEMENT

Reservation life was hard for native people. Many reservation homes had no electricity or running water. People suffered from serious sicknesses, especially alcoholism and diabetes. Most people had only completed five years of school, and they had few opportunities to find jobs that paid well. With an average life expectancy of just 44 years in 1970, American Indians had a death rate that was more than one-third higher than the rest of the U.S. population.

Formal **resistance** to these conditions began during World War II. The National Congress of American Indians (NCAI) formed in 1944 to protect American Indian land rights and improve educational opportunities for native people. This was the beginning of what would become the American Indian rights movement.

This photograph shows tribal representatives at a 1944 meeting of the National Congress of American Indians. The men pictured all attended the Carlisle Indian School. Today, the NCAI is the oldest and largest American Indian and Alaska Native organization.

Ex Carlislers'
National Congress of American Indians
Denver, Colo. Nov. 15-16-17-18-1944

MOVING TO THE CITY

Poverty and unemployment were a reality for American Indians living on reservations. In 1952, the U.S. government launched the Urban Indian Relocation Program. The program encouraged Indians to move to major cities to find jobs. They were promised housing, money, job training, and other resources. However, the housing was poor and there were fewer jobs and educational opportunities than they'd been led to believe.

Life in cities was very different from life on the reservations, and many American Indians had a hard time adjusting to their new environment. They felt homesick for their families and culture. American Indians also experienced racism and discrimination nearly everywhere they went. In some cities, police targeted public places where many American Indians gathered.

The police in this picture are preventing protesters from entering the Custer County Courthouse in South Dakota. Violence and discrimination by police is called police brutality. These native people are protesting the punishment of a white man for the murder of a Lakota man.

FIGHTING BACK

Tired of the discrimination their people had experienced, American Indians formed activist groups to fight back. From 1957 to 1959, the Tuscaroras of New York blocked the state government's attempt to turn their reservation land into a reservoir, or man-made lake. Tuscarora women led much of the resistance, blocking the construction equipment with their bodies and removing **stakes** that had been placed into the ground.

In 1961, the National Indian Youth Council formed. Known for their **militant** behavior, members of this group organized protests, demonstrations, and marches. This group was the first to use the phrase "Red Power." This was inspired by the Black Power movement, which was a movement around the same time that fought for rights and political power for black people.

Throughout the 20th century, states in the Pacific Northwest attempted to ignore treaties that granted native people the right to hunt and fish on and off reservation land. In the 1960s and 1970s, many American Indian groups exercised their treaty rights through "fish-ins," during which they disobeyed fishing laws. In this 1966 photograph, Indian fishermen catch salmon during a fish-in on the Nisqually River in Washington.

Civil Disobedience and Civil Rights

The 1950s and 1960s were a time of change in the United States. American Indians, African Americans, women, and other minority groups who faced discrimination began fighting for civil rights and equality. Many groups practiced civil disobedience, which is peacefully refusing to obey laws. This includes nonviolent protests, marches, sit-ins, hunger fasts, and more. Fish-ins are a form of civil disobedience. Important civil rights leaders, such as Mohandas Gandhi and Martin Luther King Jr., preached this method.

THE AMERICAN INDIAN MOVEMENT

In cities, American Indians of different backgrounds united to talk about their ideas and beliefs. Soon, they banded together in the spirit of political activism.

The most well-known activist group was the American Indian Movement (AIM). It was founded by Dennis Banks, George Mitchell, Clyde Bellecourt, and Eddie Benton Banai in Minneapolis, Minnesota, in July 1968. The group worked to address problems American Indians faced, including discrimination in the courts and denial of their treaty rights. However, AIM's first job was to do something about the police brutality and racism in Minneapolis. AIM members followed Minneapolis police officers and filmed them as they attacked and arrested American Indians. AIM members worked to make sure that Indians were treated fairly by police officers or to help them avoid police altogether.

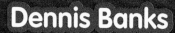

Dennis Banks

Russell Means

Dennis Banks and Russell Means were important leaders of the American Indian Movement.

FIGHTING TO BE HEARD

The American Indian Movement grew quickly. Around 200 people attended the first meeting in Minneapolis. By 1970, AIM membership had grown to 5,000. There were 79 chapters by 1973. It was now a national organization.

As AIM grew, it expanded its activist efforts. It hosted marches, protests, and sit-ins. Its attorney helped American Indians with legal issues. The group worked to improve housing for American Indian people and helped families move. The group started a radio program and a newsletter and the leaders presented programs at conferences. In 1972, AIM helped found community schools in Minneapolis and Saint Paul, Minnesota. The Heart of the Earth Survival School and Red School House were environments where students could learn about Indian culture. These programs worked to improve the lives of American Indians.

Centuries of discrimination and prejudice meant that American Indians faced hardships that placed them at a severe disadvantage. Activist groups like AIM worked to lift their people out of these **circumstances**.

OCCUPYING ALCATRAZ

In 1969, a Mohawk man named Richard Oakes organized a group of American Indians and nonnative supporters to take over Alcatraz Island in San Francisco Bay. On November 20, a group of about 100 activists arrived on the island and symbolically claimed it for the American Indian people. The occupation ended on June 10, 1971.

What Happened at Alcatraz?

The occupation of Alcatraz Island lasted for 19 months. While efforts to establish organization and leadership on the island began early in the occupation, the group became harder to control as time went on. The leadership became unorganized, some of the original protesters left, and there was fighting among the people on the island. Additionally, the government cut off the island's electricity and freshwater supplies. Stories of violence and theft were reported in the news, and the occupiers soon lost much of their support.

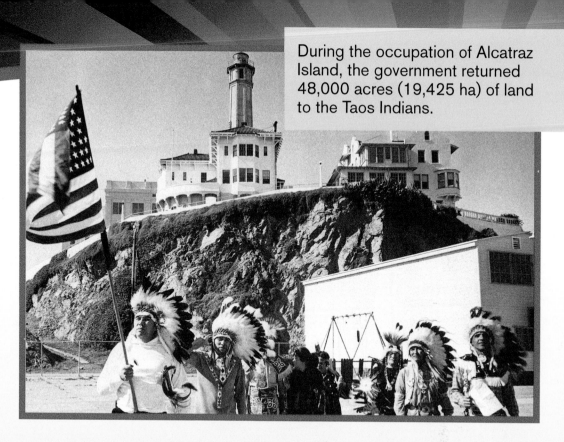

During the occupation of Alcatraz Island, the government returned 48,000 acres (19,425 ha) of land to the Taos Indians.

The occupiers had a few goals in mind. They wanted the **deed** to the island, which had been occupied by native people for thousands of years before it became part of the United States. They also wanted to create an American Indian university, museum, and cultural center. Ultimately, they wanted to show the world that American Indians needed **self-determination**. Today, American Indian self-determination is an official government policy.

THE TRAIL OF BROKEN TREATIES

One of AIM's major goals was to force the United States government to comply with, or follow, the treaties it signed with American Indian nations. On October 23, 1972, American Indian activists gathered in Minneapolis and created a list of demands to present to the government. The Twenty Points, written mostly by Hank Adams, stated that Indians wanted complete ownership and control over tribal lands.

AIM members traveled to Washington, D.C., in what they called the Trail of Broken Treaties. When they arrived, government officials wouldn't meet with them. On November 2, 1972, they seized the Bureau of Indian Affairs building and occupied it for six days. The occupation brought national attention, both positive and negative, to the cause. The protesters received $66,000 for travel costs, and the government said it would read their Twenty Points document.

These two men are standing watch at Wounded Knee, South Dakota, in 1973. This armed occupation of the Pine Ridge Indian Reservation resulted in the death of two Native American men and several injuries.

Wounded Knee II

In the 1970s, political unrest broke out on the Pine Ridge Indian Reservation in South Dakota. A group of traditional Lakota people wanted a tribal leader to step down. They called on AIM members to occupy the village of Wounded Knee, which they did on February 27, 1973. This resulted in a standoff—and shootout—between AIM and federal law enforcement. This event occurred near the site of the Wounded Knee Massacre, which resulted in the death of more than 150 Lakota at the hands of the U.S. military on the Pine Ridge Indian Reservation in 1890. The occupation ended May 8, and the negative press cost AIM a lot of public support.

THE FIGHT CONTINUES

AIM and other American Indian activist groups fought hard for change. Because of their work, important legislation was passed, such as the Indian Civil Rights Act (1968), Indian Education Act (1972), and Indian Health Care Improvement Act (1976). They turned a national spotlight on American Indian people and the issues their communities face. Their work influenced policy change at the federal level.

But the fight still continues. Until there is a society in which people of all cultures, religions, and races are treated equally, activist groups will still work to draw attention to their cause. It is the responsibility of all Americans to fight for the rights of American Indians. One day, American Indians may find that the the lands that were originally theirs have become a united nation that practices equality, acceptance, and justice.

Wearing traditional clothing to protests is a way some people show pride. This man is peacefully protesting an addition to the Keystone Pipeline System. This addition, called Keystone XL, threatens sacred American Indian land between Canada and Missouri. President Barack Obama rejected the Keystone XL Pipeline proposal in 2015.

TIMELINE OF THE AMERICAN INDIAN RIGHTS MOVEMENT

1778
The U.S. government begins a policy of making treaties with American Indian nations.

1800s
Thousands of American Indians are forcibly removed to reservations west of the Mississippi River.

1944
The National Congress of American Indians forms.

1952
The U.S. government launches the Urban Indian Relocation Program.

1960s–1970s
American Indians exercise their treaty rights through protests called "fish-ins."

July 1968
The American Indian Movement forms in Minneapolis.

November 2, 1972
American Indian activists take over the Bureau of Indian Affairs building in Washington, D.C., during the Trail of Broken Treaties protest.

October 23, 1972
American Indian activists gather in Minneapolis to write the Twenty Points protest document.

1978
American Indian activists organize the Longest Walk to raise awareness about Indian civil rights.

GLOSSARY

activist: Someone who acts strongly in support of or against an issue.

ancestor: Somebody who comes before others in their family tree.

anthropologist: Somebody who studies the history and ways of life of people.

circumstance: A situation, or the way things are.

complicated: Having many parts.

culture: The beliefs and ways of life of a group of people.

deed: A legal document showing ownership of land.

mascot: A person, animal, or other thing that is a symbol of a group or team.

militant: Aggressive in support of a cause.

minority: A group of people who are different from a larger population in some way.

resistance: The refusal to accept or comply with something.

self-determination: The process by which a nation determines its own statehood and forms its own government.

stake: A strong wooden or metal post driven into the ground in order to mark something.

treaty: A formal agreement between two groups of people.

INDEX

WEBSITES

Due to the changing nature of Internet links, PowerKids Press has developed an online list of websites related to the subject of this book. This site is updated regularly. Please use this link to access the list: www.powerkidslinks.com/civic/airm